THE KACHARI KINGDOM

RAJYA BIHIN RAJKUMAR

Contents

CHAPTER I

Introduction

The **Kachari Kingdom** (called **Dimasa Kingdom** in medieval times) was a powerful kingdom in medieval Assam. The rulers belonged to the Dimasa people, part of the greater Kachari ethnic group. The Kachari Kingdom along with other kingdoms (like Kamata & Sutiya) are examples of state formations among the Kachari ethnic groups that developed in medieval Assam in the wake of the ancient Kamarupa Kingdom. Remnants of the Kachari Kingdom existed till the advent of the British and gave its name to two present districts in Assam: Cachar and North Cachar Hills (which changed its name to Dima Hasao district in April 2010). The origin of the Kachari Kingdom is clear. Some historians speculate that they were the remnants of the Mlechchha dynasty of Kamarupa Kingdom. According to tradition, the Kacharis or Dimasas had to leave the Kamarupa Kingdom in the ancient period due to political turmoil. As they crossed the Brahmaputra river some of their compatriots were swept away down river and came to be called Dimasa or *Dima-basa*, sons of the great river Dima, the Dhansiri river. It is conjectured that the initial state formation began in the Sadiya region (coterminous with the later Sutiya Kingdom) because the Dimasas and the Sutiyas have a common tradition of the worship of *Kechai Khaiti*, the goddess in Sadiya.

CHAPTER II

The Kachari Kingdom at Dimapur

By the 13th century, the Kachari Kingdom extended along the southern banks of Brahmaputra river, from Dikhow river to Kallang river and included the valley of Dhansiri and present-day Dima Hasao district. According to the Buranjis, the Kachari settlements to the east of Dhansiri withdrew before the Ahom advance. The Sutiya Kingdom existed further east and the Kamata Kingdom to its west.

CHAPTER III

The Kachari Kingdom at Maibang

At Maibang, the Kacharis kings came under Brahmin influence. The son of Dersongphaa took a Hindu name, Nirbhay Narayan, and established his Brahmin guru as the *Dharmadhi* that became an important institution of the state. The king's genealogy was drawn from <u>Bhima</u> of the <u>Pandava</u>s, and his son <u>Ghatotkacha</u> born to <u>Hidimba</u>. The kingdom then came to be known as Heramba, and the rulers Herambeswar.

The king was assisted in his state duties by a council of ministers (*Patra* and *Bhandari*), led by a chief called *Barbhandari*. These and other state offices were manned by people of the Dimasa group, who were not necessarily Hinduized. There were about 40 clans called *Sengphong* of the Dimasa people, each of which sent a representative to the royal assembly called *Mel*, a powerful institution that could elect a king. The representatives sat in the *Mel mandap* (Council hall) according to the status of the *Sengphong* and provided a counterfoil to royal powers.

Over time the *Sengphongs* developed a hierarchical structure with five royal *Sengphongs* though most of the kings belonged to the *Hacengha* clan. Some of the clans provided specialized services to the state ministers, ambassadors, store keepers, court writers and other bureaucrats and ultimately developed into professional groups, e.g. *Songyasa* (king's cooks), *Nyablasa* (fishermen).

By the 17th century, the Kachari rule extended into the plains of Cachar. The plains people did not participate in the courts of the Kachari king directly. They were organized according to *khels*, and the king provided justice and collected revenue via an official called the *Uzir*. Though the plains people did not participate in the Kachari royal court, the Dharmadhi guru and other Brahmins in the court cast a considerable influence, especially with the beginning of the 18th century.

CHAPTER IV

The Kachari Kingdom at Khaspur

The region of Khaspur was originally a part of the Tripura Kingdom, which was taken over by Chilarai in the 16th century. The region was ruled by a tributary ruler, Kamalnarayana, the brother of Chilarai. After the decline of Koch power, Khaspur became independent. In the middle of the 18th century, the last of the Koch rulers died without an heir and the control of the kingdom went to the ruler of the Kachari Kingdom. After the merger, the capital of the Kachari Kingdom moved to Khaspur, near present-day Silchar.

CHAPTER V

Neighboring states

<u>Chilarai</u> attacked the Kachari Kingdom in 1562 during the reign of Durlabh Narayan and made it into a tributary of the <u>Koch Kingdom</u>. The size of the annual tribute – seventy thousand gold *mohars* and sixty elephants – testifies to the resourcefulness of the Kachari state. A small colony of Koch soldiers, who came to be known as *Dehans*, enjoyed special privileges in the Kachari Kingdom. A conflict with the <u>Jaintia Kingdom</u> over the region of Dimarua led to a battle and the defeat of the Jaintia king (Dhan Manik).

After the death of Dhan Manik, Satrudaman the Kachari king, installed Jasa Manik on the throne who is said to have manipulated events to bring the Kacharis into conflict with the Ahoms once again in 1618. Satrudaman, the most powerful Kachari king, ruled over Dimarua in <u>Nagaon district</u>, North Cachar, Dhansiri valley, plains of Cachar and parts of eastern Sylhet. After his conquest of Sylhet, he struck coins in his name.

CHAPTER VI

Hostilities with Ahoms

The Ahoms settled into the tract between the Sutiya and the Kachari Kingdoms that was inhabited by the Borahi and Matak peoples. The first clash with the Ahom Kingdom took place in 1490, in which the Ahoms were defeated. The Ahoms sued for peace, and an Ahom princess was offered to the Kachari king and the Kachari took control of the land beyond the Dhansiri. But the Ahoms were getting powerful and pushed the Kacharis back west. In 1526 the Kacharis defeated the Ahoms in a battle, but in the same year they were defeated in a second battle. In 1531 the Ahoms advanced up to Dimapur, the capital of the Kachari Kingdom or Hirmba Kingdom, removed Khunkhara, the Kachari king, and installed Detsung in his place. But in 1536 the Ahoms attacked the Kachari capital once again and sacked the city. The Kacharis abandoned Dimapur and retreated south to set up their new capital in Maibang. Maibang is Dima Kachari origin dialect. Mai means Paddy and bang means Plenty or aboundance. Then Maibang- a plenty of paddy.

CHAPTER VII

British Occupation

After Gobinda Chandra, the British annexed the Kachari Kingdom under the <u>doctrine of lapse</u>. At the time of British annexation, the kingdom consisted of parts of Nagaon and Karbi Anglong, North Cachar, Cachar and the Jiri frontier of <u>Manipur</u>.

Towards the south of the Nagaon district, surrounded by the river Jamuna and Hariajan, Barail Hills, Dhansiri river, Dimarua, Buri-Ganga, there was a small independent kingdom of 1800 sq. miles area. During British take over of Assam, here ruled the last lion of the Thaosena Dynasty, whose name was Tularam Senapati. Now everybody has forgotten his name but once upon a time everybody was afraid of his determination, mental power, courage, adventure and physical strength. He was a terror to his enemies. There was a saying that even the wild elephants were afraid of Tularam.

The Kacharis have a close blood relation with the Assamese people, which can never be denied. The Dimasa, branch of the Kacharis call themselves as the progeny of the river Brahmaputra.

Halali, the original name of the Kundil Nagar of Sadiya, was given by the Kachari-Chutiya residents of that time.

Although the Kacharis have the same one origin, they are sub-divided into many sub branches. The main branches which contributed immensely to the creation of an unique culture in the Brahmaputra valley are - Bodosa, Dehan, Lathaosa, Fonglongsa, Thaosens, Hammusa.

The historical stories of the Hammus branch had enriched the Assamese Literature. The Dehan or the Dhyan Branch had come from the extreme east of Upper Assam. "Tejimola, Pansoi, Kachonmati, Fulora-Sotola. Lokhai-Tora" etc., all the legendary folk tales have come from this branch of the Kachari people. So, the history will give evidence more than 100 times that the Kacharis are the architect of the back-bone of the Assamese Culture.

Tularam Senapati belonged to the Thaosen branch of the Kachari tribe.

The main royal cook of king Krichna Chandra, the last independent King of Cachar, was Kasi Chandra. People of the same dynasty, having the same blood in his vein, could only become a chief cook in the royal kitchen. In that way, cook Kasi Chandra and the king Krichna Chandra, others were close relatives, by being from the same dynasty. Tularam Senapati was the son of this royal cook Kasi Chandra. Although, Kasi Chandra, belonged to royal dynasty, some people used to look down at him as only a cook of the king. But Krichna Chandra placed Kasi Chandra at a higher platform as he was a relative of the King.

After Krichna Chandra, his son, Gobinda Chandra became the King. Gobinda Chandra, was a puppet in the hands of the British.

The British were planning to take over Cachar, at that time and Gobinda Chandra preferred to stay under the protection of the British. The British saw their opportunity and slowly progressed in that line.

Tularam, could forsee this and was unhappy. As he was also from the royal family, like Gobinda Chandra, he also demanded a separate kingdom for himself from the British. Although Kasi Chandra, father of Tularam, was a royal cook. Many people knew that he also belonged to the ruling royal family and so the people respected Kasi Chandra very much and held him in high esteem. King Gobinda Chandra did not like this at all and out of jealousy, he had Kasi Chandra, secretly murdered.

Tularam was furious on hearing about the murder of his father and determined to take revenge for this cowardly act of Gobinda Chandra. Tularam was absolutely mad with anger.

Tularam, started visiting every family and pointed out to them how Gobinda Chandra was licking the boots of the British, and how he was leading the whole Kachari tribe to slavery of the British. Thus Tularam convinced all the people of the Kachari tribe against Gobinda Chandra and also against the British. And as a result, David Scott the first Commissioner of Assam under the British, was scared of Tularam and so he instructed Gobinda Chandra, to hand over a part of his country to Tularam Senapati. Gobinda Chandra at first did not agree to the proposal of the British and his oppression on his subjects increased further. Tularam took advantage of this situation and a revolution was about to start against Gobinda Chandra and the British. Now the British got really very scared and David Scott was very much worried. Then Scott gave a strict order to Gobinda Chandra, "You have been constantly quarrelling with Tularam Barman of your kingdom. Tularam has occupied some areas of your country with due permission from us. Your people must not enter in those areas. And you too do not create any problem anywhere for Tularam."

After intervention of David Scott, an area of 2224 sq. miles, taken out of Cachar and was given to Tularam, where he started ruling independently. The kingdom over which Tularam ruled was sorrounded by the Kopili river, Bhotiya

Gaon, Samsai Gaon and Jatinga.

Tularam, assumed the title of Barman and ruled over this small kingdom independently from 1829 to 1834 A.D.

The British with their "divide and rule" policy, applied to the simple natives, were reducing the area of Tularam's kingdom. On 3rd November 1834, Tularam, had to make a treaty with the British representative, by which the area of Tularam's kingdom was reduced. The original area of 2224 sq. miles was reduced to 1800 sq. miles. Slowly Tularam's health was deteriorating and he started living at Kachamari. Over there, he left this world on 12th October 1850.

Tularam, was a very intelligent and bold man possessing all the qualities of an able king. He was also very sincere and religious man. He constructed several temples at Kachamari and his wife Dhanavati wrote a book of songs named "Dipok."

Tularam was a sincere Hindu King as evident from the names of his granddaughters and daughter in laws, which were as follows - Rohini, Bisakha, Gobindi, Sarada, Indra-Prova, Mondodari, Baneswari etc. His language was Assamese, his culture was Assamese and he was a disciple of an Assamese Guru.

The story of Tularam is still remembered by the Bodosa and Dimasa Kacharis who believe that another hero like Tularam will never be born in the whole Kachari tribe.

As doubted by Tularam, after the death of Gobinda Chandra, the British took over Cachar after his death.